The
MAGIC
MAN

by Larry Strauss

Lowell House House
Juvenile

Contemporary Books
Chicago

The L.A. Forum crowd salutes Magic as he breaks Oscar Robertson's all-time assist record near the end of the 1990–91 season.

For Ray—hang in there, man.
—L. S.

Acknowledgments
Thanks to Hal Unterberger and Hadrian Lesser for research assistance and to Lisa Melton for editing with her heart as well as her pencil.

Photo Credits
cover and page 2: courtesy of Stephen Dunn/Allsport
pages 16, 38, 67: courtesy of UPI/Bettmann
pages 21, 63, 70, 75: courtesy of AP/Wide World Photos
pages 34, 52: courtesy of Focus on Sports, Inc.

Designed by Debora Whitehouse
Manufactured in the United States of America

ISBN: 0-929923-98-7   Library of Congress Cataloging-in-Publication Card No.: 92-106
10   9   8   7   6   5   4   3   2   1

Table of Contents

June Bug Becomes Magic

"Without these two beautiful people, I wouldn't be here. The Magic makers. . . . I know both of them are sitting at home right now, my dad probably in his favorite seat, the same one where he used to tell me and explain to me how to really play this game. If you're listening Dad, I just want to thank you and tell you that I love you so much. And tell Mom I love her, too."

— **Magic Johnson, center court at the Great Western Forum, on the night he broke the all-time NBA assist record**

Lansing, Michigan, is not a magical place. It is a pretty ordinary town of about 100,000 people. They make Oldsmobiles in Lansing. Like any other town in the region, Lansing has hot and humid summers. The winters are cold, very cold, with lots of snow, wind, ice, and slush.

Christine and Earvin Johnson, Sr., raised seven children in a modest home in an average working-class neighborhood of Lansing. Even the name of their street—Middle Street—was about as ordinary as you can get. Earvin, Jr., was the middle child, born on August 14, 1959. That year,

Bill Russell and Bob Cousy led the Boston Celtics to their second National Basketball Association (NBA) title over the Western Conference St. Louis Hawks. Back then the Hawks—now the Atlanta Hawks—played in St. Louis, and St. Louis was in the Western Conference. There were no Los Angeles Lakers yet; the Lakers played in Minneapolis and that was as far west as the NBA went.

The Johnsons were a close family. There were three brothers—Quincy, Larry, and Earvin—and four sisters—Lily Pearl, Kim, and twins Yvonne and Evelyn. Like children in any family, they did not always get along, but they were taught from an early age to love and respect one another no matter what. Earvin, Sr., worked on an assembly line in a factory that made Oldsmobile car bodies. He also worked different second jobs to support the family. At first he pumped gas, and later he hauled trash. Christine Johnson had a job as a school custodian. Earvin, Jr., dreamed of making enough money so that his parents would not have to work so hard.

He was a happy child with a special glow. His first nickname was Junior, but he was later called "June Bug" because he was stout and his father thought he resembled the fat little insects that cover the ground in June! According to one of his teachers, Earvin had that "magic" smile long before he had the nickname. She recalled how he and some friends got together to sing and dance their imitation of the Jackson Five. Earvin loved music. He learned to play bass guitar, and for a while his mom thought he would pursue a career as a musician. Earvin never lost his love of music—to this day, music gives him inspiration—but his dreams of being a famous musician were soon replaced by dreams of playing professional basketball.

Earvin's love of basketball began when he was nine. On weekend afternoons in the winter, when the chilly wind rattled the windows, his father set aside time to watch the NBA game of the week with him. Earvin, Sr., had played basketball in high school and knew the game well. He'd grown up on a sharecropper's farm in Mississippi but later moved, with his mother, to Chicago. He'd had a hard life, but didn't complain about it. He just wanted his children to have it better than he had. His fondness for hoops became a common bond between him and Junior.

Those hours of watching and cheering and talking about the subtleties of the game with his father were very special to Earvin, Jr. When Earvin's dad could, he would come to watch Junior play his first competitive games for his elementary school. Sometimes, father and son would play one on one. Magic has never forgotten the time they spent together, and he gives the credit for his success as a basketball player to his dad.

Earvin was quick to learn the skills of dribbling, passing, shooting, and rebounding. By age eleven he was almost six feet tall and was the best player in his school, the star of the Main Street Elementary team. He carried a ball with him almost everywhere he went and could be seen dribbling his way to school each morning. When stuck inside on rainy or snowy days, he would ball up freshly washed socks and take jump shots at an imaginary hoop on the wall. When he wasn't practicing, he was dreaming about what a great player he would be some day—in junior high, in high school, in college, maybe even in the NBA!

One day when he was in the fifth grade, his dreaming

got a little carried away and he forgot to do an important assignment. Earvin's teacher, Mrs. Dart, wouldn't let him play in his next game—which was for the fifth grade championship. Earvin was devastated. He went home and asked his mother to do something. He pleaded with her to talk to Mrs. Dart on his behalf, but Earvin's mom believed very strongly in the importance of education. She believed that no matter what special talents a person had, an education was essential to having the greatest opportunities in life. She stood behind Mrs. Dart 100 percent.

It was a harsh punishment, especially for someone who had looked forward so much to that game and had such a passion for winning big games—but at the same time it helped Earvin to put basketball in perspective and to learn to keep his priorities straight. Earvin realized that Mrs. Dart had disciplined him because she cared about him. The two became very close, like family. In fact, Mrs. Dart's husband gave Earvin his first job (delivering ginger ale). Years later, when Magic won his third Most Valuable Player (MVP) trophy, he dedicated it to Mr. and Mrs. Dart.

Earvin never missed another game because of failing to do his schoolwork. He responded to his mother's emphasis on education by being a good student. He did his homework every night, and every morning he woke up early to practice shooting hoops on his school playground. When it snowed, he brought a shovel with him. In the summer, he played basketball all day every day—except for Sunday mornings, when his mother took him and his brothers and sisters to church.

Earvin attended Dwight Rich Junior High School in his neighborhood for grades seven, eight, and nine and played on their basketball team. By age fourteen, he was six feet, five inches tall and was a dominating player. His hard work and practice paid off, giving him his first encounter with fame. One morning, a friend showed Earvin the sports page of the newspaper and pointed to a tiny item. It said, "Earvin Johnson scored 26 points to lead Rich Junior High to victory." Earvin was thrilled. He didn't let it go to his head, though. He just thought, *Wow, I'm in the newspaper!* and let the good feeling motivate him to work even harder.

His reputation grew with each game. Sports fans all over Lansing were expecting him to be a great high school basketball player.

** ** **

In the summer of 1974, with Earvin about to enter the tenth grade, he was all set to play for his neighborhood high school, Sexton High. For years, he had watched the team and dreamed about wearing their uniform, stepping out onto their gymnasium court, hooping it up for friends, family, and neighbors. Most of his friends would be going to Sexton. They'd have a great time! But as Earvin would soon find out, things weren't going to work out that way.

In Lansing, just as in many American cities, most white people lived in one part of town and most black people in another. Few neighborhoods were very integrated. To try and integrate public schools, many cities and states instituted mandatory busing. In most cases, that meant black students rode buses to schools in white neighborhoods. Earvin Johnson was one such student.

Earvin worried when he found out he'd be bussed across town to mostly white Everett High. His two older brothers, Larry and Quincy, had been bussed to Everett High a few years before, and they had told Earvin stories of racism and even violence. But Earvin decided to try to make the best of the situation. If there was ever going to be an ambassador of goodwill and harmony, he decided it would be him.

Everett High's basketball team hadn't had much of a reputation, but Earvin was determined to change all that. It is rare that a sophomore makes the high school varsity basketball team, but Earvin was a rare player. He not only made the varsity in his first year at Everett, but had a good chance to make the starting five. Earvin was anxious to prove himself, to show his new teammates that it was winning time! But he was also nervous. His brother, Larry, had been cut from the Everett High team some years ago and told Earvin it was because he was black.

As the Everett High Vikings suited up before the first practice, none of the white players spoke to Earvin. He ran out on the court ready to win them over with his ability. But when Coach Fox called for a scrimmage, none of the white guys on Earvin's squad would pass Earvin the ball. They froze him out.

Earvin complained to the coach, but Fox didn't want to hear about it. Earvin had never before encountered anything like this, and he didn't know how to handle it. Fortunately, he had help. Not only were his parents behind him, but he was also fortunate enough to have a very important mentor—a grown-up who cared about him and gave him good advice.

Dr. Charles Tucker was a former junior college All-American basketball player who had played some pro ball but had never really made it. He had later become a psychologist. Earvin had met him in junior high school when "Tuck," as Earvin called him, had come to talk to Earvin's class about responsibility. The two had hit it off because of their common interest in basketball, but Tuck's influence on Earvin went much further.

After that first Vikings practice, Tuck had a talk with Earvin in the locker room. He got Earvin to step outside his own situation and see things objectively. He told him not to assume that these white guys were freezing him out because he was black. He said it was envy, not bigotry, that caused the other players not to pass him the ball. It had been *their* team; *they* had been the stars, and here was this new guy who was about to show them up and take over. Part of being a true team leader, Earvin discovered, was realizing that not everyone thought the way he did. Other guys had their egos and if you didn't deal with that, you couldn't really come together as a team. Before long, the Everett High Vikings did unify as a team, with Earvin as the leader.

Earvin had some differences of opinion with Coach Fox about the way the game should be played. Fox was wary of Earvin's behind-the-back dribbling and his no-look passes, but Earvin convinced the coach that these tricks weren't just for show: they were a way to fool a good defender.

Earvin got off to a somewhat disappointing start in his first high school game. His coach and many of the fans had spent a lot of time bragging to other coaches and fans about Earvin. Even though he played just fine—twelve points with a few rebounds and assists—it was a big letdown for many. However, for Earvin the main thing was that the team had won. From the second game on, Earvin lived up to the hype. He baffled defenders with his ability to snatch a rebound and dribble through traffic "coast to coast"—from one end of the court to the other—and then dunk the ball in someone's face. He stunned coaches and lit up the nylon nets. In one game, he had thirty-six points, eighteen rebounds, and sixteen assists—and before long, he had a new nickname.

Fred Stabley, a sportswriter for the *Lansing Star Journal,* approached Earvin in the locker room one night after a game. Stabley, who likened Earvin to spectacular Philadelphia 76ers superstar Dr. J, asked Earvin what he thought of "Magic." Earvin liked the sound of it. The next morning, he saw the words "Earvin 'Magic' Johnson" in Stabley's article. Soon, all the local writers were using the nickname. Earvin never imagined that it would become his trademark, his identity, but when the sportswriters began to drop his first name, he found himself becoming simply "Magic" Johnson!

Earvin's mother didn't like the name. She was a deeply religious woman who believed that a person's talents and abilities came from God. She expressed her feelings to Earvin, who assured her that it was only a nickname and wasn't intended to mean any disrespect toward God. Earvin, Sr., was also concerned about the name, and he warned Earvin that it would not be easy to live up to it. Magic assured his dad that he was prepared for the task.

That year, 1975, Everett High finished with a record of 22–2 and made it to the state quarterfinals, against Fordson Dearborn High School. Everett came out and dominated Fordson for three quarters, building up a thirteen-point lead. But in the last ten minutes, Magic's team faltered. They missed free throws, letting Fordson chip away at the lead and eventually overtake them for the victory. It was Magic's hardest defeat. He blamed himself for the loss because two of the missed free throws had been his. After the game, he wept. The loss haunted him for a while, but it also helped him to begin coping with the fact that "you can't win 'em all." The pain of losing helped him learn to be a gracious winner—to think of how the other guy feels and not to rub it in. But most of all, Magic let the loss inspire him to improve, to work with his teammates to make something positive come out of their loss.

During the spring and summer of 1975, Magic practiced hard on his game. His friend Tuck coached him in some of the finer points of the game. He took Earvin to Michigan State University (MSU) to watch the Spartans play, and took him to Detroit to compete on the inner-city playgrounds and to watch the NBA Pistons play. Tuck even took Earvin to the pro locker rooms after games and introduced him to some of his idols, such as Kareem Abdul-Jabbar. When Earvin shook hands with "the Big Fella," he got so excited that he looked at his own hand with amazement. Tuck assured Magic that one day he would give that same kind of thrill to thousands of kids.

Magic was like a sponge, learning about basketball and improving his abilities whenever he could. He would hang out in the gym at nearby Michigan State and watch the college players scrimmage against each other. He studied the way they played. One day, the seven players on the floor needed another man to have a four-on-four game. They hollered to the kid in the stands. Magic responded, and his playing earned him the respect of the older, more skilled players. One of the MSU players, Terry Furlow, took Magic under his wing. It wasn't long before the 16-year-old Magic even found himself playing summer games with such NBA pros as George Gervin. Magic was amazed to be on the same court as Gervin, eye-to-eye with such a great player. In these summer games, it didn't matter so much who you were as what you could do on the court. Gervin was awesome, but Magic held his own—as did his crosstown rival, future NBA player Jay Vincent.

Magic and Jay, who were about the same age, played for different schools and loved to compete against each other. They later played on the same college team, and much later they found themselves on the same Laker squad for part of a season.

** ** **

Magic's junior year in high school was the first time he played guard. Most guards are small, quick players who can handle the ball well and make long-range shots from twenty feet and beyond. At more than six feet, six inches, Magic was taller than many high school *centers*, but he could handle the ball and shoot as well as any other guard. In the backcourt, he was able to have an even greater effect on the game. From that position, he controlled the ball. He could take an outside shot, drive to the basket, or pass to an open man. Because he was so tall, he could look over the heads of his opponents and see all his teammates, wherever they were. Defenders never knew what he was going to do. He was unstoppable.

Everett lost only once during the regular season. They

made it to the state semifinals before suffering another painful defeat, this time at the hands of Detroit Catholic Central. Again, Magic felt responsible for the loss—and this time he had company. Everyone at Everett High, it seemed, had something to say about the way Magic "blew" the game. He'd played *too* unselfishly, passing the ball when he should have shot. It wasn't easy to hear all that criticism, but with the love and support of his mom and dad, Magic learned to accept criticism as part of the game.

Magic's family and friends also helped him stay focused on his priorities. Despite all the attention he was getting for his basketball abilities, Magic still hit the books. He maintained a B-minus average and even found time to work on the school newspaper. He never assumed that basketball would be the only skill he'd need to make it in the world.

And though his long-term future looked more promising every day, he concentrated on the immediate. He knew he would go on to play in college and would have a shot at pro ball, but for the time being his goal was to get to the state high school basketball championship in his last year at Everett. He wanted it for himself and for his teammates, most of whom would not have another chance at glory in college or the NBA.

Magic was awesome his senior year for the Vikings. The sportswriters who cover high school basketball voted him a preseason high school All-American, and he lived up to that status.

This time, Everett made it to the state finals against a school called Brother Rice. The game was at the Chrysler Arena at the University of Michigan, Ann Arbor. The place was huge, and there wasn't an empty seat in the house!

From down on the hardwood floor, it seemed as though the Vikings and their opponents were surrounded by every basketball fan in the state. Their cheers and foot stomps pounded like the nervous heartbeats of the players. The pressure was on.

It was a tough game. It went down to the wire and into overtime. This time, Everett didn't fold in the crunch, and Magic led the team to victory.

It was a sweet win—all the more so because of the agony of defeat in previous attempts at the championship. For Magic Johnson, it was only the beginning.

Highlights of Magic's High School Career
Everett High, Lansing, Michigan

- First Team Michigan All-State Player (1976, 1977)
- Michigan State High School Championship (1977)

Magic drives past Indiana State's defense during the 1979 NCAA basketball championship.

All-American

"Every team I've played on was not supposed to win. Even when I go to the playground, I don't pick the best players. I pick the players who want to work hard."
—**Magic Johnson**

Like most high school stars, Magic Johnson's involvement with the collegiate game began long before he put on a college team uniform. Since the time of his sophomore year at Everett, he was one of the most sought-after prospects in the nation, receiving letters and phone calls from recruiters representing schools all over the country—from the University of Maryland to the University of California at Los Angeles (UCLA). Magic was elated. Colleges he had only dreamed of playing for now wanted him! He knew, though, that what the recruiters really cared about was not him or his future, but the future of the college teams they represented.

It was spring of 1977. With his dad and Dr. Tucker, Magic spent long hours learning the rules and regulations of National Collegiate Athletic Association (NCAA) recruiting. He learned what was legal and what was not, so that when he was illegally offered money, cars, and other favors, he knew immediately to say "No thank you." Magic knew that if he just kept on working hard and playing straight, the money would eventually come the right way.

Being offered athletic scholarships by nearly all the top schools in the country—including Notre Dame, North Carolina, and UCLA—made it difficult to choose, but eventually Magic narrowed it down. During his high school days, Magic had grown used to having the support of close friends and family at his games and in his life. He didn't want to put too much distance between himself and the people he loved. So he decided to choose one of the two universities closest to home: the University of Michigan or Michigan State University.

Deciding between the two was no easy matter. The University of Michigan, in Ann Arbor, had a more impressive basketball reputation. Its team, the Wolverines, had made it to the 1976 NCAA championship game. Previous Michigan greats included Cazzie Russell and Rudy Tomjanovich. By contrast, Michigan State's team, the Spartans, hadn't won its conference championship—much less an NCAA title— since 1959, the year Magic was born. But it was right in Lansing. Not only would this make it possible for Magic's friends and family to attend all his games, but it would also enable Magic to give something back to the community—

namely, an NCAA championship.

He chose Michigan State. In an interview around that time, Magic said, "The Wolverines were on national TV and this and that. But I like the underdog school."

** ** **

Magic loved college life. His longtime competitor and friend Jay Vincent had also chosen MSU and the two shared a dormitory room. Magic was a campus sensation before he ever set foot on the basketball court. To his amazement, everywhere he went other students as well as professors stopped him to say hello and shake his hand. He couldn't wait for basketball season to begin.

Michigan State plays in the Big 10 Conference, one of the most competitive in college sports. The school's rivals include such basketball powers as Indiana, Michigan, Ohio State, Purdue, Illinois, and Minnesota. In 1977 Magic had to compete against such future NBA players as Mychal Thompson, Kevin McHale, Randy Whitman, and Herb Williams. In Magic's first week of conference play he averaged 25.5 points, 5 assists, and 7.5 rebounds per game and was named Big 10 Player of the Week. More important to Magic, he helped the Spartans win. During the week of January 23, 1978, Magic's picture appeared for the very first time in *Sports Illustrated,* along with words of praise for his game and for his magnetic personality. Meanwhile, Magic was earning top grades with a 3.4 grade-point average at the end of his first semester (no small feat for *any* college freshman).

Under the guidance of Coach Jud Heathcote, the Spartans won the Big 10 Conference title, earning them an automatic entry into the NCAA tournament. It was Magic's first year of college and already he had a shot at the national collegiate championship! The championship tournament is called "March madness," because it takes up most of that month and fans everywhere watch teams from every corner of America compete against one another. It's "do or die"—win and you play the winner of another game, lose and you go home. The tournament began with forty teams (today it has expanded to sixty-four), playing at various sites around the country. Finally, the best four teams converge in one place to determine which team will be number one.

Magic and the Spartans were confident as they took the floor in Indianapolis on March 11, 1978, for their first game in the Mideast Regional. MSU defeated the University of Providence (Rhode Island), 77–63, and Magic had fourteen points and seven assists despite a sore ankle. The team then beat Western Kentucky, 90–69. The Spartans' next opponents were the University of Kentucky Wildcats, ranked number one in the nation. The Spartan underdogs weren't intimidated. Although the Wildcats were a powerful squad, featuring such future pros as Kyle Macy and Rick Robey, the Spartans had the Magic Man.

Magic got off to a slow start, missing his first few shots. But he kept his teammates involved, and late in the first half he made a nice move to the basket for a slam dunk, helping Michigan State to a 27–22 halftime lead.

In the second half, however, the Wildcats made some adjustments. They played a zone defense, with each Wildcat guarding a part of the court rather than another player. One or two Wildcats always stood near the basket to keep

Always smiling, Magic talks to a referee during the 1979 NCAA championship game. Looking on is Indiana State's Larry Bird.

Magic from scoring or receiving passes. Coach Heathcote told his team to slow down and hold onto the lead. The Spartans played too cautiously, however. Magic learned the hard way that you cannot protect a lead—certainly not for an entire half. You have to keep playing the kind of game that got you the lead in the first place. The Wildcats picked their game up a notch. The Spartans didn't, and they lost by three points, 52–49. The season was over. Magic was frustrated and disappointed, but he didn't point fingers at his coach or at anyone else. It was a team loss, and Magic made sure everyone understood that.

He finished his first year of college with a solid B average and looked forward to the next season. In the fall, he made it into *Sports Illustrated* again, but this time he was on the cover! National collegiate basketball polls of sportswriters rated the Michigan State Spartans one of the top ten teams in the country. Some sportswriters were even picking the Spartans to win the NCAA title.

Unfortunately, MSU got off to a horrible start, losing half of their first eight conference games. They were nearly out of the running for the Big 10 title. Unless they pulled it together fast, they might not even get into the NCAA tournament at all. The same sportswriters who had praised Magic only a month before were now blaming him for the team's slump. Magic tried even harder, but it seemed to him as though nothing he did helped.

His friend Tuck caught up with Magic in the gym early one morning, and they had a talk. Tuck helped Magic to quit paying so much attention to what was being written about him. The problem, Magic began to realize, wasn't that he didn't do enough. It was that he was trying to do *too* much. He had assumed responsibility for the entire team, and he was trying to do everything himself. Tuck encouraged Magic to be the team leader he was capable of being. This included speaking to the coach in a diplomatic way about the team's concerns.

Working together, the Spartans turned things around

and salvaged their season. Magic turned up his charisma and put the fun back in the game—for everyone except their opponents. Michigan State won nine of their next ten conference games and miraculously finished in a tie for the Big 10 title. They were on a roll going into the NCAA tournament.

This time, the tournament selection committee placed them in the Midwest Regionals. MSU's first game was against the Lamar University Cardinals from Texas. The Spartans dominated, winning the game 95–64. Despite losing a key player in that game—Jay Vincent went down with a stress fracture in his foot and was out for the rest of the tournament—the team went on to defeat Louisiana State University, 87–71, then Notre Dame 80–68. That earned Michigan a ticket to Salt Lake City for the Final Four.

In Salt Lake City, the media were everywhere—the hot lights, the microphones, the questions. The world was watching. Magic kept his composure and displayed his charm, but he kept his focus on what he'd come for: to lead his teammates to victory.

Michigan State's semifinal opponent was the University of Pennsylvania, the first Ivy League team to make it to the semifinals in more than ten years. But that was as far as Penn was destined to make it. By halftime, Magic and his supporting cast had run and gunned to a 50–17 lead. The Spartans scored a record 101 points and won by a record margin of thirty-four. Magic wound up the game with twenty-nine points, ten rebounds, and ten assists, and he left the floor hugging his teammates with the realization that they were going to the championship game—and were just one win away from their dream!

And Larry Bird stood squarely in their way. The six-foot, ten-inch star had his sights set on the same goal as Magic. Bird and his Indiana State Sycamores came to the finals with a 33-game winning streak. On April 30, 1979, the Magic/Bird era of basketball began.

The two stars knew and had some respect for each other. Of Magic, Bird said, "He is more of a passer and I'm more of a scorer." But Bird also saw similarities. Both he and Magic had a problem with making passes so spectacular that their own teammates couldn't catch them.

In what became the highest-rated NCAA final to date, the Michigan State Spartans tipped off against the Indiana State Sycamores. The game was close for the first five minutes. Then Michigan State took the lead when Magic got the ball to guard Terry Donnelly, who made a basket. Magic was his usual spectacular self. On one play, he grabbed a rebound and dribbled upcourt. He seemed to slow down—but only long enough for the defenders to relax. Then he stepped up the pace and drove past the Sycamores for a lay-up.

But it wasn't the Spartans' offensive flair that made the difference for them. It was their defense. The Spartans did what no other team had done: they stopped Larry Bird. During MSU practices, Magic had pretended to be Larry Bird, playing all his moves, until his teammates figured out how to stop Larry Bird himself.

During the game, Bird kept calling for the ball, but his teammates couldn't get it to him, and when they did he couldn't get off good shots. When it was over, Magic was hugging his teammates and Bird was sitting sadly on the bench. Magic had won the first round of their rivalry, but both players had much to be proud of. They had taken losing teams and made them into the best and second-best teams in the country. Bird was named College Player of the Year by sportswriters and coaches, and Magic was the runner-up. And they would meet again in the NBA.

Magic would be one of five players voted First Team All-American by sportswriters. But for Magic, the greatest accomplishment of that year would always be winning the NCAA championship for the hometown fans.

Magic's future looked very bright indeed. He was only nineteen years old, having a wonderful time as a student-athlete, and NBA teams were already interested in him. Magic had a decision to make.

Highlights of Magic's College Career
Michigan State University, Lansing

- 1978: Big 10 Conference Champions
  Second Team All-American
- 1979: Big 10 Conference Champions
  NCAA Champions
  NCAA Tournament MVP
  First Team All-American
  Runner-Up College Player of the Year

STATS:

Season (year)	Games played in	Field Goal%	Free Throw%	Rebounds (per game)	Points (per game)
77–78	30	.458	.785	237	17.0
78–79	32	.468	.842	234	17.1
Totals	62	.463	.816	471	17.1

College or the Pros?

"College basketball is fun. What's better than that?"
—Jay Vincent, Magic's college teammate

"Opportunity comes once."
—Dr. Charles Tucker, Magic's friend and advisor

"Two more years . . . Two more years . . ." chanted the Michigan State fans at a pep rally in honor of their NCAA championship basketball team. No, they weren't demanding that the Spartans win the trophy in 1980 and 1981—only that Magic Johnson play for them through his senior year. As one MSU fan put it, "Every member of the team is a hero, but Magic is a legend."

The Los Angeles Lakers might not have thought Magic was a legend, but Coach Jerry West (soon to be general manager) and the rest of Laker management believed he was one incredible player. They had been hoping to add to their team one player who could rebound and another who could handle the ball. Magic could do both! The Lakers had the number-one pick in the 1979 NBA draft, and they wanted Magic.

Magic, his father, and Tuck had many strategy sessions about what to do. Finally, they decided to at least talk to Laker owner Jack Kent Cooke. Though the draft was several weeks away, the Lakers had made it clear that they would draft Magic if he would leave college early and play for them.

NCAA rules did not allow Magic to have a lawyer accompany him to his meeting in Los Angeles, so his advisors were his dad and Tuck. The three flew to Los Angeles and got themselves a room in a motel near the L.A. Forum. Los Angeles was a strange place to Magic—a huge city of palm trees and mountains and freeways. In Lansing, people drove big American cars. In L.A., people cruised around in Mercedes, Jaguars, BMWs, Toyotas, and Datsuns.

The next day they met in the Forum Trophy Room with Cooke, Jerry West, Laker radio and TV announcer Chick Hearn, and other Laker insiders. Cooke was a brilliant businessman. He was slick, polished. But Magic wasn't intimidated. He was confident that he'd win no matter what he decided. He told Cooke that he wanted to be the highest-paid rookie in the history of the NBA. If not, he'd definitely go back to Michigan State.

Cooke tried to bargain, but Magic stood firm. And he won—the first of many negotiating triumphs for Magic the businessman. The Lakers offered Magic a guaranteed contract for more than half a million dollars. This made his decision all the more difficult.

As he left Los Angeles and flew back to Michigan, Magic had not decided what he would do. He understood the importance of a college education. If he forgot it for one minute, his parents (especially his mom) were there to remind him. But he also understood the risks of injury. If he got seriously hurt during his last two years of college, he could lose his lifelong dream of becoming a pro. Besides, he knew that many NBA players who leave college before graduating go back during the off-season, or even after retirement, to finish their education. Some even go on to get graduate degrees.

But there were other considerations. For one, Magic was reluctant to leave home. He was used to the warmth and enthusiasm of a hometown crowd. All over Lansing, people urged him to stay. Kids, especially, got to Magic. When a little boy at a nearby schoolyard worriedly asked Magic if he was going to leave, Magic almost cried, realizing how much he meant to so many people. Of course, Lansing didn't have an NBA team, and so he would eventually *have* to leave to pursue a pro career. But he had hoped he could play for the Detroit Pistons or the Chicago Bulls. That way, he could come home on the weekends when he wasn't on the road. Also, Magic was concerned about playing in Los Angeles. He had heard that L.A. had mean big-city sportswriters and unenthusiastic fans.

Mostly, Magic saw his difficult decision as a choice between two tremendous opportunities. He was having a great time at Michigan State, and he had a chance to win back-to-back NCAA championships and complete his college education. Yet the Lakers had much to offer. They had

Kareem, and a chance to play with "the Big Fella" didn't come around every year. With the Lakers, Magic would have a good shot at winning a championship during his first couple of seasons in the NBA.

Magic knew how lucky he was to have such a decision to make. "Heck," he told one reporter, "I remember when I couldn't even let myself dream about being all-city. Then all-state was out of the question, because of all those great guys out of Detroit." Now, he could choose either to be the NBA number-one draft pick or to be an almost sure-thing All-American player for the second year in a row!

With all the love, support, and advice Magic had, he still had to make a decision for himself. His mom wanted him to finish college, but she wouldn't tell him what to do. His dad wanted Magic to decide what *he* most wanted to do. When it came time to finally make up his mind, Magic couldn't help thinking about his parents and how much they had given him. It wasn't only his own future he was concerned about. He wanted his dad to stop working two jobs and wanted his mom to take it easy.

Magic became a Laker—and with his first paycheck, he bought his parents a new house in Lansing.

A Magical Rookie Season

"I have never seen or played with anyone like that—a superstar of that caliber who actually would practice every day. And the practices were just as competitive and intense as the world championships."
—**Jamaal Wilkes, about Magic Johnson**

Magic began his pro career during the Los Angeles summer league, a series of exhibition games for NBA rookies and other players who want an opportunity to demonstrate their abilities to pro scouts, assistant coaches, and a few die-hard fans. The games were held in the gym at California State University, Los Angeles. Normally, these summer games would draw a few hundred spectators. But when word got out that Magic Johnson would be playing, the place was sold out.

When Magic got into the game, the fans went wild.

Magic smiled and waved at the crowd, thinking about how everyone had told him that L.A. fans never got excited! Then he gave them something to *really* get excited about. He snatched a rebound and speeded downcourt before the defenders could set up. It was the first of hundreds of Magic-led Laker fast breaks. He drove toward the basket, as if he had one and only one intention—to score. Then, at the last second, he sent a no-look pass to a teammate for a lay-up. The next time down, he faked out a defender and drove for a dunk shot. It was *showtime!*

The summer of 1979 was an exciting time both for L.A. basketball fans and for Magic, who was an instant celebrity. But at the same time, Magic missed his family and friends. He missed his old neighborhood. For the first time in his life he wouldn't see the sidewalks covered with leaves in autumn or snow in winter. He wouldn't taste his mother's cooking for a while. He had never lived alone, and now he had his own apartment. He was having the time of his life—and feeling the pangs of homesickness.

Magic also felt the pressure of being a highly paid, highly touted rookie. Jack Kent Cooke talked to Magic about what it meant to wear the purple and gold. The Lakers were a team with a long, proud, and also frustrating history. Since moving from Minneapolis to Los Angeles in 1961, the Lakers had been to the NBA Finals nine times and had won the championship only once, in 1972. The team Magic joined in 1979 had a lot of talent, but it hadn't been able to put all the pieces together. They were counting on Magic to help them do just that.

Magic took on the challenge. NBA players are much tougher, stronger, and more physical than college players.

It is easy for a rookie to get pushed around, especially in training camp, where some of the other players are trying to make the team. But Magic's mentor, Tuck, had prepared him, and Magic was ready to muscle with the veterans. Magic had to adjust to not being the star of the team. He had worn number 33 in high school and college, but on the Laker team he gladly deferred to Kareem, who already wore 33 for the Lakers. As if out of respect for the Big Fella, Magic subtracted a digit to become number 32. He played his heart out and impressed veteran All-Stars like Kareem, Jamaal Wilkes, and Spencer Haywood. They chuckled about Magic's excitement. They had never seen so much talent and enthusiasm in one player. He was a rookie, and they figured it would wear off.

The Lakers' first regular-season game, on October 12, 1979, was against the Clippers, who were then playing in San Diego. As had happened in high school and college, Magic got off to a bad start. His first quarter was terrible. Magic missed most of his shots while the guy he was guarding, Lloyd Free, kept scoring. But Magic didn't panic. Instead, he gathered himself and focused on the moment, on what he could do for the team.

During the second quarter, Magic came on strong. With the Lakers down by fifteen, he scored seven points and had two assists to spark a Laker comeback. Toward the end of the fourth quarter, Magic had scored twenty-six points and had shown that he was ready for the NBA, but his performance wouldn't matter to him unless the Lakers won the game. With only a few ticks on the game clock, the Clippers were ahead 102–101, but the Lakers had the ball. Kareem threw up a sky hook at the buzzer—and it went swish through the net!

The Lakers had won. Magic went wild as though they had just won the championship! He jumped toward Kareem, landing in his surprised teammate's arms with a feverish embrace. Kareem, the epitome of cool composure, was stunned—but after a moment he couldn't keep from cracking a smile.

Magic's love of the game was contagious.

During the first weeks of the season, Magic averaged more than twenty points per game and his enthusiasm scored a victory with his teammates. Soon, the Lakers were winning with regularity and enjoying it. Opposing players and coaches were beginning to respect, and even grow fond of, Magic Johnson. Said Brian Taylor, an opposing guard, "He really *is* magic. He's got great charisma . . . What makes Magic special is the way he brings his own personality to it." Magic was not an "in-your-face" kind of player, one who would go out of his way to show up an opponent. Other players appreciated that and respected him for it.

But they weren't sure how to defend him. No one had ever seen a six-foot, nine-inch point guard before. Players that tall weren't supposed to be able to dribble more than a few feet, much less bring the ball upcourt or run a fast break to perfection. Guards weren't supposed to be able to compete for rebounds with centers and power forwards. What Magic brought to the NBA was more than a winning attitude. It was a whole new way of playing the game of basketball.

It was a long, exciting season for Magic. Every rookie has to make adjustments to be successful in the pros, and

Magic was no exception. He was playing with and against the best players in the world. There were very few easy games. But Magic made the most of every moment.

Sometimes, walking through an airport in a strange city with a pair of Walkman headphones on, he would stop in

Magic Johnson and Kareem Abdul-Jabbar led the Los Angeles Lakers to five NBA championships in eight years.

the middle of the terminal, singing out loud and dancing. People would stop and stare. By the end of the season, Magic's celebrity status was nationwide. He'd been chosen to endorse 7-Up and Converse sneakers. His signature was on Spalding basketballs, and he was making public relations appearances for the big hometown company, Oldsmobile. This meant having to deal with the public wherever he went, keeping his composure even when fans did not. But most important, he had to keep his mind on basketball.

The Lakers had an awesome year. They overtook the defending champion Seattle Supersonics to become the top team in the Western Conference. For most teams, winning fifty games in a season is great (the all-time record is 69–13). But the Lakers finished the 1979–80 regular season with a 60–22 record, the best in the league. Attendance at Laker games was way up. L.A. fans were excited, and suddenly, Angelenos were like Magic's hometown fans.

The playoffs began in late April. The Lakers defeated the Phoenix Suns, then the Seattle Supersonics, and moved on to the NBA Finals against the Philadelphia 76ers—and Dr. J.

It was a best-of-seven match, which meant that the first team to win four games would be the champions. It was a tough, hard-fought series. The Lakers won the opening game at the Forum, but then the Sixers took the second game. The series moved to Philadelphia, where each team again won one game. This set up a crucial game five back in L.A.

It was a close game all the way. Toward the end of the third quarter, with the Lakers clinging to a two-point lead, Kareem went down with an ankle injury and had to leave the game. The crowd was stunned, and so were the Lakers.

Magic stepped up. He took control of the offense, made some big hoops, and made even bigger assists to get the other Lakers involved. Soon the Laker lead was eight. The Lakers held off the Sixers until Kareem came hobbling back onto the court during the fourth quarter. The fans went wild. Magic and the other Lakers were inspired by the courage of the Big Fella, who played on his bad ankle. With 33 seconds left to play, Kareem scored the winning basket, and the Lakers won 108–103.

But Kareem's ankle would keep him out of game six, scheduled to be played in Philadelphia. In the meantime, Laker Coach Paul Westhead decided to start Magic at center. Magic knew this was a great opportunity for him, and he decided to make the most of it. He had fun with the idea of replacing Kareem for one game. When the Lakers boarded the plane to Philly, Magic sat in Kareem's seat. He joked that he was going to play like Kareem.

That night—May 26, 1980—Magic jumped center for the Lakers against the much bigger Caldwell Jones. He lost the tip-off but did not despair. When the Lakers got the ball, he played the center position as though he'd played it his entire life. He stood near the foul line, with his back to the basket, playing the high post position the way Bill Russell used to do it. He found Michael Cooper free and whizzed him the ball for a score. Back on defense, he grabbed a rebound, then became a guard again long enough to dribble the ball to the other end of the court and make a ten-footer. Soon after, he drove around Sixer star Dr. J and went up toward the basket, as if to dunk. Sixer big man Darryl Dawkins got in his way and stuck his hands up, ready to swat away Magic's shot. Magic faked the dunk, and when Dawkins went for the fake, Magic—still in mid-air—tossed the ball over Dawkins' outstretched fingertips for a basket.

Magic just blew the Sixers away. He played center, forward, and guard. He scored forty-two points and pulled down fifteen rebounds to go along with seven assists, three steals, and a blocked shot. Other Lakers, inspired by his performance, also played great.

"It was one of the most awesome individual performances I've ever seen," Dr. J said later. When it was over, the Lakers were the champs, with no seventh game needed. Magic and his teammates embraced at center court but they waited until they got back to L.A. for the real celebration with their proud captain, Kareem.

Magic became only the third basketball player in history (along with Bill Russell and K. C. Jones) to win NCAA and NBA championships in consecutive years. He was voted by a group of sports journalists as the MVP of the finals. It was the first time a rookie had ever won that honor.

The Rookie of the Year award went to Larry Bird by one vote. As had happened when they were in college, Bird won the personal award while Magic won the championship. That was fine with Magic; he'd take winning anytime.

Just three years out of high school, Magic had already had a spectacular basketball career. He looked forward to spending the summer back home in Lansing, taking summer classes at Michigan State, playing softball and singing on street corners with his old friends. And there was always next season to look forward to. It seemed as though the winning and the good times would never stop.

In the 1987 NBA Finals, Magic Johnson and Larry Bird battle for the ball in one of the most exciting championship series in NBA history.

Challenges and Heartbreaks

"Sometimes . . . you don't want to be Magic at all."
—**Magic Johnson**

The moment Magic was hit, his knee felt strange. It was 1980, on a November evening in Atlanta, and Magic was under the Hawks' basket. All seven feet, two-and-a-half inches of Hawk Tom Burleson had just fallen on Magic.

When Magic got up and walked around, his knee didn't hurt very much, so he kept playing. A few games later, he got banged by another big bruiser, Tom LeGarde of the Dallas Mavericks. Magic felt pain and heard a strange clicking in his knee. He was able to run, though, so he continued to play through the pain. Then the Lakers moved on to Kansas City, where Magic's knee simply *stopped*. It happened during the second quarter. Magic was on defense. The player he was guarding, Hawkeye Whitney, made a sudden move toward the basket. Magic reacted, trying to stay with him—and something in his knee snapped.

The next thing Magic knew, he was back in Los Angeles on an operating table. It was only his second season, and his entire pro basketball career was in the hands of sports injury surgeon Dr. Steve Lombardo!

The operation was declared a success, but Magic would have to remain out of the game in a cast for several months. No one knew for sure if he would ever be the same great player again. Magic had depended on his quickness and agility, his ability to run, to fake, to spin. If his knee did not fully recover, he could lose his edge.

Magic tried to keep a positive attitude. This was made easier by the support of his family and of Tuck, who all flew out from Michigan to be with Magic as he recuperated. Magic tried to keep things light. There was no sense in getting down about something he couldn't do anything about.

After a while, though, he began to feel frustrated. Ever since he'd started playing ball, he had never gone more than a few days without running the court. He got restless sitting around in his apartment, waiting for his leg to heal. He missed the camaraderie of the team, hanging with the guys, having fun. He joined the Lakers on the bench for a few games and cheered them on to some victories.

After several weeks, the cast was taken off, and the painful rehabilitation of his knee began. Magic worked hard. He had to get his endurance back. Running had never been his favorite pastime, but now he had to run more than

ever before. Tuck helped him to understand the serious-
ness of the situation and gave him the hardest workouts of
his life. He had Magic sweating and panting and dizzy—and
asking for more. Magic realized that before he could put his
number 32 back on, he would have to be in top form.

It wasn't until late February that Magic got the nod
from the doctors and Laker owner Jerry Buss to start
playing again. Magic's return was a home game on February 27, 1981, against the New Jersey Nets. He wondered
how the fans would react. He'd missed forty-five games.
The team, after stumbling for a while, had done alright
without him, and had a 28–17 win/loss record. The Nets
were not a very good team that year, so Magic thought
there might not be much of a crowd.

But the game was a sellout with 17,505 fans in the
stands, many of them wearing buttons that said "The
Magic Is Back." The fans gave Magic a long standing ovation. Magic just stood there with his usual brilliant smile.
He opened his arms, as if to say, "What did I do to deserve
this?" Reporters from all over the country converged on
the Forum to witness Magic's return.

When the game tipped off, Magic was on the bench,
but with five minutes left in the first quarter he entered the
game to the roar of the crowd. His skills were rusty. His
first pass was easily intercepted, and his second pass went
out of bounds. His first two shots looked awful. But he
hung in there, and in the fourth quarter, with the Nets
closing the Laker lead to just 103–98, he showed that
the magic wasn't gone. He faked out his opponent, then
whipped a perfect pass to teammate Norm Nixon, who
sank a fifteen-foot jump shot. Then, at the very end of the

game, Magic snatched an offensive rebound that preserved a two-point lead. By the final buzzer, he was well on his way back to form. But more important, the Lakers had the win.

In the locker room afterward, Magic tried to give as much credit as he could to his teammates, who had kept the Lakers winning in his absence. But reporters would have no part of Magic's modesty. It was Magic-mania for weeks and weeks. When Magic's teammates were interviewed, most of the questions were about his recovery. It was difficult for them not to resent all the attention Magic was getting.

Though he didn't let on, Magic felt he was *not* playing his usual best. He knew it would be a while, if ever, before his knee felt really good, but it simply wasn't his style to make excuses.

He also felt out of step with his teammates. They'd been playing without him for months and had grown used to filling the gap he left. One night, he and Norm Nixon got their signals crossed and ran into each other. Magic not only felt this awkwardness on the court, but in the locker room and on the team bus as well. Out of step. Sometimes the guys would make a joke he didn't get because he'd been away. It was like being a rookie again, only worse because of all the attention he got from everyone outside the team.

But Magic kept a positive attitude and felt confident that things would work themselves out. In the next few months, the Lakers managed to get their game up a notch. Then, just as the playoffs neared, a misunderstanding erupted between Magic and teammate Norm Nixon. Nixon supposedly told a newspaper reporter that Magic was hogging the ball and the spotlight. When reporters asked

Magic for a response, he made a big mistake. He let his emotions get the best of him and he responded without first talking to Norm. He said, "We've become a bunch of individuals," meaning that the Lakers were no longer getting along as a team. "Everybody spends more time worrying about getting his share and what the other guy is getting than about winning." Had Magic talked to his friend first, they might have worked things out. But he hadn't.

Magic's words were printed in all the local newspapers. This public statement angered Norm, but worst of all, it destroyed the Laker team morale. Before they knew what hit them, the Lakers were on the verge of being knocked out in the first round of the playoffs.

The Lakers were tied 1–1 in a miniseries with the Houston Rockets (in what is now a best-of-five but was then a best-of-three series). Fortunately, the Lakers still had home-court advantage for the deciding game. It turned out to be a close contest. With just thirty seconds left in the final quarter, Magic got fouled and went to the line for two free throws—and missed them both! The Lakers were down by one point, but they still had a chance to win the game.

Magic controlled the ball as the game clock wound down. He was supposed to pass the ball to Kareem as soon as the Big Fella positioned himself in the right spot near the basket. But Houston Rocket center Moses Malone wouldn't let Kareem get positioned, so Magic drove toward the basket himself. He made a pretty spin move around two Rocket defenders and took the potential game-winning shot.

The ball left his hands. It rose, it arced, it fell toward the basket—and it came up short. An air ball.

The season was over. Magic had blown the big game and didn't even have the camaraderie of Norm Nixon and other teammates to fall back on. The next morning the newspapers came down hard on Magic. They said that he had not only missed a crucial shot but had choked under pressure. One of the more bloodthirsty reporters even gave him a new nickname: "*Tragic* Johnson."

Magic was devastated. It was as if all his accomplishments were forgotten. All anyone could remember was one bad shot.

Magic's family helped to cheer him up. So did Jerry Buss, who brought Magic and Norm Nixon together to clear the air and renew their friendship. More than that, Buss showed Magic that he hadn't lost confidence in him, and that meant a lot to Magic. Buss made it clear that he wanted Magic to be a Laker for life. He offered Magic an incredible twenty-five-year, $25-million contract. Magic couldn't wait until the next season to show that he was worth every cent.

By the beginning of the 1981–82 season, Magic's knee was 100 percent, but the Lakers still got off to a bad start. Not only did they lose a lot of games, but they played without any of their usual "showtime" flair. Magic and some of the other Lakers felt that Coach Westhead's offensive scheme was too complicated. Magic, never shy about talking to the coach, appointed himself spokesman and told Westhead of the team's complaints. Westhead insisted that he had a good offensive strategy, and that if Magic would be patient, things would work out.

But the situation grew increasingly tense as the Laker team continued to stumble. Magic and Westhead continued to clash. Magic wasn't used to losing on a consistent basis. But more than that, he wasn't used to the *way* the team was losing. For Magic, basketball had always involved hard work, but it also was always fun. That was no longer the case with the Lakers. By mid-November, Magic was thoroughly frustrated. After a road game in which they barely beat the Utah Jazz (who weren't a good team that season), Magic told some reporters that he wanted to be traded. "I can't play here anymore," he said. "I want to leave . . . I'm going to talk to 'the Man' and ask him to trade me."

According to Jerry Buss, Laker management had already decided to fire Westhead and was just waiting to find a replacement before making it official. But Magic, by venting his frustrations through the media, had made it seem as if he had forced Buss to fire the coach. It created a panic situation, with no one sure who the coach was or would be. Magic knew he'd made a terrible mistake—one he would never make again—but it was too late.

The man chosen to replace Coach Westhead was one of the Laker assistant coaches, a former Laker player and broadcaster who'd never been a head coach before. It was Pat Riley. He took over as interim coach and put stability back into the team. He also promised to bring back *showtime.*

Like most people in the Laker organization, Riley was not thrilled with the way Magic had handled his conflict with Westhead. But Riley was quick to forgive Magic. So were Magic's teammates.

Magic hoped the fans would also forgive him, but he knew they might not. After all, he had said he wanted to leave L.A. The Lakers' next game was at the Forum, against the San Antonio Spurs. Magic was the first player to be introduced: "At guard, six-foot-nine, from Michigan State University . . . Earvin 'Magic' Johnson!" Magic jogged onto the floor, praying for cheers—but instead receiving a long, loud round of boos.

He was devastated. His own fans seemed to hate him! He stood there, holding back the tears, thinking, *What did I do to deserve this?*

The fans' hostility continued through the first quarter. Magic knew of only one way to turn things around: play great basketball. But it was difficult to concentrate. The boos kept returning every time he touched the ball. Even when he made a sweet feed for an assist, the fans didn't cheer for him. But he didn't give up. Midway through the second quarter, he snatched a defensive rebound, ignited a fast break, and ended it with a perfect "alley-oop" pass— floating the ball up toward the basket. Michael Cooper caught the ball and slam-dunked it. Suddenly, the fans could not help but cheer. The next time down, Magic passed the ball to Kareem for a basket. Soon after, Magic drove the lane for an easy score of his own. By the second half, he'd won back the affection of the hometown fans.

NBA fans outside Los Angeles were a different story. Loyal fans always yell at the opposing team, but not the way they jeered at Magic. Some fans would boo him every time he touched the ball. Sportswriters sharpened their pens on him, saying he was overpaid and stuck-up, not the great guy everyone had thought he was.

Never before had Magic ever felt such hostility, and it hurt. But it also taught him an important and valuable lesson. The attention a person gets by being a great athlete is not the same as the love of friends and family. The fans who love you today can turn on you tomorrow—and there are some people who cannot wait for the opportunity to bring a guy down. Knowing this made Magic all the more grateful for his friends and family.

When the fans and some writers and sportscasters were back on his side, Magic wasn't bitter. He appreciated having their admiration back. But he didn't mistake it for love.

Somehow, despite all the controversy and the setbacks, Coach Riley and the Lakers not only salvaged that season but also went on to win another championship against Dr. J and the Philadelphia 76ers. And they did it with pure, unstoppable, showtime basketball. On some nights, there were so many fast breaks by the Lakers that the referees complained of exhaustion! Magic was again voted MVP of the playoffs.

** ** **

Two championships in three years had made L.A. fans expect the Lakers to do it every year. In the 1982–83 season, the Lakers won 58 games and cruised back to the NBA Finals—where they were embarrassed and humiliated, *swept* by a powerful 76ers team. Suddenly, everyone in sports was wondering whether the Lakers were fading.

The next spring, Magic and the Lakers had a chance to prove the critics wrong. Again, they made it to the finals. This time, the opponent was the Boston Celtics. It was the Magic/Bird matchup that basketball fans everywhere had been dreaming of ever since the two great stars had met in the NCAA championship game back in 1979. And that

47

wasn't all. It was *the Lakers and the Celtics,* an old rivalry heating up again. Since 1962 the Lakers and the Celtics had met seven times in the finals, and the Celtics had won all seven matchups.

In the days leading up to game one, the media began to hype the series as a showdown between the "natural talent" of the Lakers and the "hard work" of the Celtics. This did not make sense to Magic. He knew he was as hard a worker as any Celtic—and, for that matter, that Bird was not short on natural talent. But Magic had learned that the best thing to do about media hype was to ignore it: play your game and let the chips fall.

Both Magic and Bird took the same approach when, in pregame interviews, they were asked about the rivalry between them. Each player stood, sweating in his practice uniform, talking about how great the other was. Magic told reporters that to him Bird was more than a great scorer; he was a great all-around player. Bird said, "Magic is just beyond description. I think of him as one of the three top players in the game today, maybe the best. He's a perfect player."

The 1983–84 NBA Finals tipped off at the Boston Garden on May 29. Magic had an impressive game one, scoring eighteen points to go along with ten assists and six rebounds. Bird scored twenty-four points, with fourteen rebounds and five assists. But the stat that mattered most to both was the final score: Lakers 115, Celtics 109.

Magic was elated but not cocky. The Lakers needed three more wins and Magic was taking it one game at a time.

Game two went down to the wire. With less than

twenty seconds left in the final quarter, the score was tied and Magic had the ball. He was dribbling it near the three-point circle, waiting for the clock to wind down so that he could get the ball to Kareem for the last shot. If he made it, the Lakers would be 2–0 in the series and would have a good shot at a four-game sweep.

But the buzzer sounded before Magic had a chance to pass the ball to Kareem or anyone else. The Celtics would now have a chance to win in overtime.

It looked to fans as though Magic just hadn't been watching the clock. In fact, he had not had the right pass opportunity at the right moment. Had he thrown a bad pass for an interception, it could have turned into a disaster. It was a team mistake, but Magic took the heat when the Celtics won (124–121). It was one thing to miss the last shot, and another to fail to even *get* a shot.

Still, the Lakers were in a good position with the series tied 1–1 and game three back in Los Angeles at the Forum. Magic had a superior game, and the Lakers blew the Celts out of the building, 137–104, to take a 2–1 lead in the series. But that lead was soon forgotten.

Game four, also in L.A., was an undeclared war. The Celtics used physical play and intimidation to slow the Lakers down, and it worked. The Lakers stood up to the Celtics, but in fighting back they got out of their rhythm.

The game went down to the wire. Just as in game two, Magic had the ball and a chance to win with the last shot of the game. Again, he didn't have a good pass to make—but this time he passed the ball anyway. The ball was stolen, and the Celtics almost scored. The game went into overtime, and again Magic found himself in a high-pressure situation. He got fouled and went to the line for two free throws that could tie the game—and he missed them both. The Celtics won the game 129–125 and Magic blamed himself. Had he taken care of business, he thought, the Lakers could have swept the series. Instead, they had to return to Boston for game five.

The game was held on a hot, humid Friday night at the Boston Garden, an ancient arena with no air-conditioning. It was a sauna, and game five turned into an endurance test. Some of the Lakers even slipped in turns at an oxygen tank during time-outs to get their energy back. The Celtics, who were more accustomed to playing under such conditions, prevailed, and won 121–103.

Magic and the Lakers had their backs against the wall as they returned to L.A. for game six. Although Kareem had to play with a migraine headache, the Lakers won 119–108. Magic had a solid game, helping rookie Byron Scott to a great shooting performance. But he knew no one would remember any of that unless the Lakers could go back to Boston and win the deciding game.

Game seven was a classic battle between basketball's two best teams in a *must-win* situation. The Celtics led most of the way, but the Lakers hung tight. Magic had an off game that night. He had picked an awful time to have a shooting slump, but he found other ways to help the team.

Late in the fourth quarter, with one minute, fourteen seconds left on the clock, the Lakers had pulled to within three points (105–102). Magic had the ball and drove to the basket, but Celtic center Robert Parish stole the ball from Magic and ignited a fast break. A four-point switch! That was, as they say, the nail in the coffin. The Celtics won the game 111–102 and were the champions.

It was the low point of Magic's career. In the locker room after the game, he was so depressed that he wound up sitting on the floor of the shower, covered with soap, talking with Michael Cooper and trying to figure out what had gone wrong.

When he returned to L.A., Magic locked himself away from all but his closest friends. The newspaper headlines had no sympathy. Again, they said he had choked. "EARVIN, WHAT HAPPENED TO THE MAGIC?" asked the *Los Angeles Times* one morning. Magic couldn't answer. Critics said he lacked heart—that he could win when it was easy but that when the pressure was on in a close game he couldn't come through. The cruel nickname "Tragic Johnson" resurfaced.

Magic and his teammates had just played in one of the greatest, hardest-fought NBA Finals ever. The Celtics deserved the championship. Magic had set an NBA Finals record of ninety-five assists!

For two years in a row and for four out of his five years as a pro, Magic had made it to the finals—an accomplishment some players never achieve *once*. But none of that seemed to matter to the fans and sportswriters. With all the bad press Magic was getting, he might as well have been on the last-place team.

Alone, with the awful memories of his on-the-court mistakes replaying over and over in his mind, Magic wondered what he would have to do to prove himself once and for all.

Known for his spectacular assists, Magic passes the ball to an open Laker teammate for a quick score.

Player of the Decade

"He really transcends the game of basketball. He does so many things for so many people on the court, and it's always been geared toward one thing . . . to win."
—**Pat Riley on Magic Johnson**

With his mom, dad, Tuck, and other close friends and family, Magic was able to put the discouragement of June 1984 behind him. Soon, his new house was filled with furniture and loved ones. In fact, Magic furnished one room especially for his mom and dad, one for Tuck, and another for his best friend in the NBA, Detroit Piston Isiah Thomas. To those whom Magic loved and who loved him, he wasn't a failure, he didn't lack heart, he hadn't choked, and he sure did not have anything to prove.

But that didn't mean he was satisfied with the way he

played. He knew there were aspects of his playing that needed improvement, and he spent a lot of his summer working on those things. He never wanted to miss another crucial free throw, so he practiced foul shots for hours and hours. He lifted weights and did other conditioning to get stronger.

All the Lakers were anxious for the next season to begin so they could prove to themselves—and to their fans—that they could rise from the ashes of last season. When the 1984–85 season began, they got off to a slow start, but eventually they came on strong. By the mid-season All-Star game, they were solidly in front in the Western Conference.

On February 11, 1985, Magic started for the Western Conference All-Stars for the fourth time. The NBA All-Star game is usually an exciting exhibition, with some of the best players strutting their stuff for a national audience. For many players, it is an honor just to be there. For Magic Johnson in 1985, it was an opportunity to show fans across the country that last year's finals had been a fluke. Magic was a man on a mission. There have been some great individual performances in NBA All-Star history, but never a great amount of teamwork since the players are from different teams and have never played together before. With Magic on the floor, though, it happened. Somehow, Magic knew when and where to get the ball to the other Western Conference players.

Magic racked up twenty-one points and fifteen assists. But once again, his accomplishments went less noticed than his mistakes had. As his friend Isiah Thomas put it: "He's at the point now where he plays great, great basketball every night and it's not even noticed."

Magic and the Lakers again steamrolled toward the 1985 NBA Finals. Magic hoped the Lakers would meet the Celtics in the championship matchup, and he got his wish.

Game one was at the Boston Garden. The Celtics were incredible, and by halftime, the Lakers had been blown out of the game. It was the most lopsided win in NBA Finals history: 148–114.

In game two, the Lakers seemed like a different team. They stepped up the tempo and were very aggressive, and they won 109–102.

Back in L.A., the Lakers took two of the next three games in much the same fashion. Magic quarterbacked the offense, played aggressive team defense, and snatched rebounds regularly. But this was Kareem's show. Abdul-Jabbar, age 38, came on with an inspiring performance. Magic and the other Lakers were proud to be his supporting cast.

Game six was at the Boston Garden. This time, with the pressure on, Magic played a virtually flawless game while Kareem hit the big shots, and the Lakers triumphed, 120–111. They were not only World Champions for the third time in the 1980s, but they had proved to everyone, once and for all, that they had heart. For Magic, beating Boston, *in* Boston, made it the sweetest championship of his pro career.

Magic kept getting better. The guy who had blown all those crucial free throws became one of the top foul shooters in the NBA. The guy whose weaknesses were defense and shooting started stealing the ball with regularity and nailing increasingly long outside shots. It used to be that defenders could let Magic have an outside shot. No more! He'd burn them—*swish!*—from two- *and* three-point ranges. As good as Magic was, what amazed people the most was that he continued to improve. He wasn't satisfied being the best guard in the league—he wanted to be even better than he already was.

Despite Magic's personal accomplishments, 1986 was not the Lakers' year. Although they had a good season, finishing with the second-best record in the league, they fell apart in the Western Conference Finals and were beaten by the Houston Rockets.

Unlike earlier years, this time no one singled out Magic as the culprit. Many people said the Laker team was simply getting old, fading. That was fine with Magic, who had always liked the underdog. Now, he and his teammates *were* the underdogs.

In the first game of the 1986–87 regular season, the Lakers played the Rockets in Houston. The Rockets won—more proof that the Lakers were history. Magic didn't like getting beaten—especially on national TV—but he knew it was only one game. He was confidence personified.

The Lakers didn't lose many after that one. Magic made sure of that. The Lakers were still Kareem's team on paper and in their hearts, but out on the court Magic was stepping up more and more and becoming the backbone of the Lakers. He could get the ball to James Worthy for a quick jump shot or a spinning dunk shot. He could put the ball in Byron Scott's hands right on the spots where Scott liked to shoot. He could get it inside to the Big Fella. And if the defense tried to double-team Kareem, Magic would swoop down the lane for a lay-up—and often was fouled for a three-point play. On fast breaks, defenders would cringe when they saw Magic driving toward them. They knew they had two choices: run at him, in which case he would make an incredible pass for an easy two, or else jump into the passing lane, in which case Magic would drive to the basket and dunk the ball. Sometimes, on Magic's fast break passes, the ball would literally disappear from view—even to television viewers—and then reappear, magically, in the hands of a dunking Laker. On a few occasions, Magic's no-look passes were so mystifying that TV cameramen lost the play and missed the shot!

Soon, the Lakers were no longer seen as underdogs but again as the team to beat in the Western Conference. There was, however, much doubt as to whether they could beat the Celtics if both teams reached the finals. And both teams did.

To get there, the Lakers had breezed by their opponents in the semifinals. The Celtics, however, had gone seven games against both the Milwaukee Bucks and the Detroit Pistons, and they were tired and battered.

The Lakers had no mercy. In game one of the finals, at the Forum, Magic and the Lakers ran a fast break every time they got the ball. The Celtics were never really in the game. In the third quarter, when Magic lofted an alley-oop to Michael Cooper (for what had become known as a *Coop-de-loop*), the CBS TV announcer said, "If this were a prizefight, the referee would have stopped it!" The Lakers won, 126–113.

The Celtics didn't give up, though. They came out primed for game two, hoping to surprise the Lakers on the Lakers' home floor, just as the Lakers had done to them two years before. The Celtics played an almost perfect first quarter, but it wasn't enough. They found themselves working hard for their points while the Laker baskets seemed to come easily. Magic raced the ball downcourt. Dribble, pass, score. Or dribble, fake, drive, dish, *dunk!* Game two was another blowout, 141–122.

In the locker room after the game, the Lakers were happy and confident, but Magic made sure they did not get *overly* confident. Michael Cooper had set a new record for most three-pointers in a finals game that night and reporters were crowded around him, asking questions, when Magic cut the interview short. *Interview us after we've won FOUR games,* was Magic's attitude. That was typical Magic. To his teammates, the bright, cheerful Magic was also Mr. Serious-Get-Down-to-Business. He didn't like a lot of messing around during practice, and he would let his teammates know about it.

Magic's concern about Laker overconfidence was right on. For game three, the Celtics were back home at the Boston Garden, and they managed to slow the pace and beat the Lakers, 109–103. Now, it was a whole new series.

If the Lakers lost the next game, the series would be tied, and the Celtics could push the Lakers to the wall in game five. It was time to get serious. Game four turned out to be one of the greatest battles in NBA Finals history. The Celtics seemed to be on the verge of blowing the Lakers out as late as the fourth quarter. But Magic led a valiant comeback, and with only a few ticks left on the clock, the Lakers wound up with the ball and a chance to win the game.

Magic had the ball. He looked for Kareem near the

basket. No way—the middle of the floor was all clogged up with Celtic defenders. The clock was running. Magic put the ball on the floor and swept toward the basket. Two seven-foot-tall shot swatters—Kevin McHale and Robert Parish—jumped out at him. They blocked Magic's passing angle to Kareem and stuck their hands in his face. Magic rose off his left foot, palmed the ball in his right hand, and put it way back over his shoulder for a hook shot—his "junior junior sky hook," as he called it. The ball sailed over the outstretched hands of McHale and Parish and through the Boston Garden net for the winning basket, 107–106. Magic had risen to the occasion and come through in the clutch.

The Celtics came back in game five to beat the Lakers convincingly, 123–108. In game six, back in Los Angeles, the Celtics outplayed the Lakers in the first half. But it wasn't enough. While the Celtics had the power of muscle under the basket, the Lakers had the power of speed. The Lakers won the game and the championship, 106–93. It was as if the old style of basketball had given way to a new era—the Magic Johnson era. It was no longer enough to be big. A player had to be mobile, versatile.

Magic was voted series MVP for the third time. And for the first time, he was voted league MVP for the regular season—only the third guard ever to win that award (Bob Cousy and Magic's idol, Oscar Robertson, were the other two).

During the Laker victory celebration, Coach Riley made his now famous guarantee that, next year, the Lakers would be the first team to achieve back-to-back championships since the 1969 Celtics. Riley made the claim to motivate the team. He knew, though, that a repeat championship would depend more than ever on Magic. Magic was not only a superstar, he was also the biggest cheerleader on the team.

During the 1987–88 season, Magic kept getting better, adding new dimensions to his game. Those desperation buzzer-beating heaves he had occasionally made started to happen more and more frequently. During the course of only a few weeks, Magic hit three shots that won or tied games in the last second. Fans learned that he had been practicing shots from half court and beyond so he'd be ready when the Lakers needed a shot like that. Magic's "junior junior sky hook" was no longer a novelty, but a potent offensive weapon. But most of all, what he kept improving on were what basketball experts refer to as "intangibles"— the things a great player does that can't be counted and often go virtually unnoticed, like the way he could control the tempo of a game or the things he'd say to his teammates to get them to play better.

That season was the second straight year the Lakers finished with the best record in the NBA. This time, though, they had a very tough time in the playoffs. The Utah Jazz and Dallas Mavericks both took the Lakers to seven games—and, again, when the pressure was on, Magic came through. The Lakers earned another trip to the finals, a chance to make good on Coach Riley's "back-to-back" guarantee.

This time the Lakers' final opponents were the Detroit Pistons. With Magic suffering from the flu and slowed down considerably, the Pistons won the first game decisively, putting the Lakers up against the wall early in the series.

The Pistons were a hungry team, led by Magic's good friend, Isiah Thomas, and veteran former Laker Adrian Dantly, who tore apart the Laker defense in game one.

The Lakers knew they had to win game two, and to do that they'd have to slow down Dantly. Magic gave Laker A. C. Green a pep talk about guarding Dantly, while Coach Riley designed a defensive strategy in which two Lakers would guard Dantly whenever he had the ball. The Lakers started game two shooting cold, but fortunately, the Pistons also had trouble finding the basket. Then Byron Scott hit a three-pointer, and Magic knew he was the man to get the ball to. Scott scored the first seven Laker points and stayed hot. The Pistons hung close, but the Lakers stayed in control of the game into the fourth quarter.

Down the stretch, however, the Pistons came back. Then Magic, despite the flu, took command. He seemed to get stronger as the game wore on. He put the ball in Kareem's hands in just the right spot for a sky hook. He drove to the basket and found A. C. Green all alone for an easy jump shot. On the Lakers' next possession, with the 24-second clock winding down, Magic cut to the basket and got fouled in the act of shooting. Finally, a pick-and-roll with A. C. Green got the Lakers two more points and put the game on ice. The Lakers won 108–96.

The Lakers and Pistons flew to Detroit for the next three games with the Pistons hoping—and planning!—to close out the series on their home floor.

As for Magic and the Lakers, it has never been easy to win on the road. But for Magic, Detroit wasn't exactly the road. It was home. Just an hour from Lansing, Detroit was a city Magic knew well. Magic did what he could to make sure the other Lakers also felt at home.

For game three, Magic got his mother to do some home cooking. A whole *bunch* of home cooking, as a matter of fact—enough to feed the whole Laker team! They could smell the home cooking as they suited up and had it to look forward to after the game.

The Lakers came out strong. Magic helped Kareem get off to a good start with an easy deuce. He got Scott on track with a fast-break basket and some open jump shots. He got A. C. Green involved in the offense to help build the young forward's confidence. It was a close game, with the Lakers up by one point at the half. Then, in the third quarter, Magic entered what is known in the NBA as "the highlight zone." He started off with a give and go for a basket. A little while later, he got a rebound and put it in high gear for a fast break and two foul shots. The Pistons were fouling hard—to make sure there were no three-point plays and to make the Lakers think twice about going to the basket. But Magic didn't think twice, and he made shots despite hard fouls.

Midway through the quarter, Magic had the ball about twenty feet from the basket. The Pistons were packing the middle, trying to force the Lakers to take outside shots. Suddenly, Magic picked up his dribble and with one hand flicked a pass that seemed to be right at the heart of the Piston defense. Only it wasn't. The ball went right past them—right through the seams—beyond ten outstretched Piston arms and into the hands of James Worthy, standing under the basket. Worthy caught the perfect bullet pass and laid it in. The Pistons and their fans were stunned. The Lakers now had a nine-point lead, and they never looked back. The final score was 99–86.

It would prove to be the pivotal game of the series. Once they regained the home-court advantage, the Lakers were able to close out the Pistons with two very close, hard-fought victories at the Forum. Magic elevated his own game and helped his teammates, especially James Worthy (who was named series MVP), to elevate theirs. It was

Magic celebrates the Lakers' consecutive NBA championships on the steps of City Hall in Los Angeles.

quite possibly the toughest series the Lakers, especially Magic, had ever played. Pistons Joe Dumars and Dennis Rodman had kept the pressure on Magic virtually every minute he was on the floor. They had been like gum on his shoes. They hadn't stopped him, but they had made him work for everything he got.

During the 1988–89 season (which was team captain Kareem Abdul-Jabbar's farewell season), Magic won his second regular-season MVP award, and the Lakers breezed to the finals for a rematch with Detroit. The Lakers lost game one in Detroit, but came back strong in game two. Then, in the third quarter of that game, Magic pulled a hamstring in his leg. The Lakers called time out and trainer Gary Vitti rushed onto the court. Magic was limping around, trying to run it off, but the pain wouldn't go away. Vitti told Magic he'd have to come out of the game. The pain in Magic's leg was nothing compared to the pain in his heart as he left his team in the throes of a close game. The Lakers lost the game, and lost Magic for the rest of the series. Being in the finals and not being able to play, having to watch the Lakers lose in a four game sweep, was one of the toughest times of his career.

But Magic bounced right back with another great season in 1989–90. A half-step slower then he once was, Magic compensated with strength, intelligence, and ingenuity.

Meanwhile, the rest of the league kept getting better every year. The Lakers weren't going to make the finals every year anymore, but everyone knew that as long as Magic was with them, the Lakers would be one of the elite teams.

After the 1990–91 season, Magic won his third regular-season MVP. *Sport Magazine* named the Lakers the NBA team of the 1980s and Magic the NBA Player of the Decade!

He'd come a long way from All-City in Lansing.

A Class Act

"Magic is the consummate pro."
—**Michael Jordan**

Magic's smile has become his trademark. That smile tells us of Magic's love of life, his appreciation for his good fortune, and his love of other people. It reminds us that hard work and great success can and should be fun. Magic is generous with his smile, as generous as he is in the sharing of his achievements. Magic credits his mom for his now world-famous grin. "People talk about my smile," Magic once said, "but hers is the original."

Magic has dedicated almost every one of his personal achievements and awards to his father, the man who worked eighteen hours a day for his family. Magic has never, for one moment, forgotten those who have helped him get where he is. And that includes not only his loved ones, coaches, and advisors, but also his fans.

In 1986, Magic started the "Magic Family" fan club, making his fans a part of his extended family. He's given a lot of young fans souvenir pairs of his sneakers, and his enthusiasm for the game and for his fans has helped to change the NBA. Players like Charles Barkley and Dennis Rodman—who get their fans involved, who might stop to give a fan a high five after diving into the seats for a loose ball—these players are carrying on a style that Magic brought to the league.

Magic Johnson also helped to bring movie and recording stars out to watch the Lakers at the Forum. He made basketball fans out of people who hardly knew about the game before 1979. And, as with his smile, Magic has been extremely generous with his celebrity status. On many occasions, he has helped struggling business owners in the L.A. community by making a guest appearance to boost business, or by lending his name and face to good causes.

Magic has raised many millions of dollars for charities, and has given generously himself. And he's given more than money. Early in his career, Magic started putting on his own NBA summer all-star game to raise money for the United Negro College Fund. Each year, the game raises upwards of one million dollars for the fund. And Magic's idea has inspired other NBA players. Larry Bird, for instance, now has his own charity all-star game. These games bring competitors together for a common cause, raising money for those in need and showing people that

At one of his basketball camps for kids, Magic demonstrates some successful defensive moves.

some things go beyond winning and losing.

Magic has also given and helped raise many more millions for such charities as the City of Hope (an organization devoted to helping people with cancer), the Muscular Dystrophy Association, and the American Heart Association. He has worked with the Special Olympics for mentally retarded children, has helped create a program in Lansing for students who have reading problems, and has volunteered for the Make a Wish Foundation, an organization that helps brighten the spirits of children who are very sick and often dying. Several years ago, one boy who was dying of leukemia said he wanted to meet Magic Johnson. Magic not only agreed to meet the boy, but also let him stay with him and be his "little brother" for an entire week.

Magic has also shown young people that his abilities extend beyond playing basketball. He set out to become one of the most successful businessmen in America, and he *has* succeeded. He not only makes commercials for many popular products, but he also has his own clothing company. Like any good businessman, Magic has a hands-on attitude toward his business dealings, making all the important decisions himself. In 1990, he went really big time by becoming co-owner of a Pepsi-Cola franchise in the Washington, D.C., area. No athlete had ever owned anything that big. No African-American had ever owned a soft drink franchise that big. Magic didn't do it just for himself; he already had enough money. He did it to show other young people, especially African-Americans, that no matter where they come from, they can succeed in anything they work hard at.

But Magic's ultimate goal was, and still is, to own his own professional sports team. Being a sports team owner is very risky. Not all teams are as successful as the Lakers. Magic could lose a good deal of his wealth on an investment like that, but he is confident.

Over the years, Magic's priority has remained steady: winning. During the 1990 preseason, people saw yet another example of that. Not satisfied with being the best player in the league, he wanted his *team* to be the best in the league, even if it meant personal sacrifice. The Lakers knew they needed a stronger bench if they were going to stay competitive in the NBA. In particular, they were looking for a player who could shoot and rebound well enough to back up Byron Scott and James Worthy. The Lakers found their man in Terry Teagle and made a trade with the Golden State Warriors to get him. However, the Lakers had just given Sam Perkins a huge contract and didn't have any more room under the league salary cap. (NBA teams are allowed to spend only a certain amount on players so that the teams with the most money do not get *all* the good players.) It seemed the Lakers wouldn't be able to sign Teagle after all. Then Magic learned about the situation. "No problem," he said, and agreed to take a pay cut so the Lakers could sign Teagle.

As passionate as Magic was about winning, he always did it with great style and sportsmanship. In other words, for Magic, winning wasn't enough. It also had to be achieved with class. Over the course of his career, Magic never lost his drive to win, but he learned to accept defeat graciously and became the personification of sportsmanship. Although he did not always agree with a referee and would argue against a bad call, he usually responded well to a good call, even if it was against him. He'd smile, or even say, "Good call."

Magic's sportsmanship was never more apparent than at the end of the 1991 NBA Finals. This was, at last, the Magic Johnson/Michael Jordan showdown—the Lakers versus the Bulls. Magic, as always, wanted to win. The Lakers didn't play well, and the Bulls did. Toward the end of the series, Magic grew frustrated. He even talked about retiring after the 1991 season. But then, when it was over and the Bulls had proved to be the best team, Magic took the loss with dignity. He wanted to be the first to congratulate the Bulls, and TV cameras saw a remarkable sight. With the champagne still flowing in the winners' locker room, a player in the losing team's uniform came in to shake hands with the winners and tell them how much they deserved it. That player was one of the winningest players in the history of professional sports: Magic Johnson.

Many fans and sportswriters saw the 1991 finals as the passing of the torch from Magic, the player of the 1980s, to Michael Jordan, the player of the 1990s. But not Magic. He stopped talking about retirement and was determined to come on strong for the 1991–92 season. He had helped the Lakers make it to the finals nine times in twelve years, and there was no reason to think he couldn't do it again.

Three and a half months later, in October 1991, Magic joined the Lakers for their trip to Spain to play in the annual McDonald's Open. He put on a dazzling show and made thousands of new fans for the NBA, at the same time serving as an unofficial ambassador of good will for his country. He looked forward to returning to Spain in a red, white, and blue uniform for the 1992 Summer Olympics.

As the Lakers flew back to Los Angeles to begin the 1991–92 season, Magic had no idea that his career as a professional basketball player would soon be ending.

On November 7, 1991, at a televised press conference, Magic Johnson makes a startling announcement.

Magic Faces His Toughest Challenge

"If I die tomorrow, I've had the greatest life that anybody can ever imagine."
—**Magic Johnson**

November 7, 1991, Great Western Forum, home of the Los Angeles Lakers:

"Because of the HIV virus that I have obtained, I will have to retire from the Lakers today." These words, uttered by Magic Johnson, startled the world. With this statement, Magic had ended what may possibly be the greatest career in the history of professional basketball.

Within minutes the news spread throughout the city, the nation, the world. People at work crowded around radios and televisions to hear Magic's momentous press conference. People shopping in department stores gravitated toward the TV sets on display. Magic was suddenly retiring. No one could believe it. No one was even sure how much longer he would live. People cried and wondered how the Magic man felt.

For Magic, the ordeal had been going on for several weeks. It had begun when the Lakers decided to take out an insurance policy on him. A lot of teams in pro sports do that when they have a player worth as much to them as Magic. Insurance companies have always required that applicants take a physical examination to make sure they are in excellent health. These days, insurance companies require an AIDS test as well.

Like most Americans, Magic had heard about the human immunodeficiency virus (HIV), the virus that eventually causes a person to develop AIDS. Magic knew that AIDS (acquired immune deficiency syndrome) weakens the immune system, the body's way of protecting itself against harmful infections and diseases. When the immune system becomes weakened by AIDS, a person can become very sick and eventually die.

Like many Americans, Magic had not really been concerned about acquiring HIV. So, when the results of his blood test came back positive for HIV, he was shocked and afraid. His first concern was for his new wife, Cookie, and the unborn child she was carrying. It was possible that they, too, were infected. Fortunately, when Cookie and the baby were tested, the results were negative.

Unfortunately, when Magic was tested again to be sure of the first results, the test said the same. He had HIV.

Magic had a lot of important decisions to make. The

first was whether to retire or not. His doctors told him that on the one hand, since he was in such peak physical condition, he was in a good position to fight the virus and delay the onset of the AIDS disease. On the other hand, the physical exhaustion of another long NBA season could wear down his body's defenses.

The doctors advised Magic to retire. Playing basketball had always been a big part of his life, but Magic's love of basketball was never greater than his love of life. Magic did not hesitate in his decision.

Magic knows it is vital that he stay as upbeat as possible, despite the tragic news. Many doctors who treat HIV and AIDS cases have found that when a patient gets really down about it, the illness can get much worse. But how do you stay happy and positive knowing you've got the AIDS virus? Knowing it wasn't going to be easy, Magic became determined to make the best of his situation. He is grateful to have found out about it early, because he is able to do something about it right away.

Another important decision was whom he should tell about his health situation, and when and how to do so. He would have to announce his retirement from basketball fairly soon, but what reason should he give? Over the years, people with AIDS have often been mistreated by those who fear the disease. Some people do not understand that it is not contagious through casual contact. As a result, some AIDS patients have been disowned by their friends and families, just when they most needed love and support.

Taking all of this into consideration, Magic made a decision. Retiring from professional basketball did not mean that he was going to stop being a team player. He could never do that. It was his nature to give an assist whenever he could, and this was his opportunity to give the greatest assist of his life. He could turn this enormous new challenge into something helpful to millions of people. He could be a symbol of hope for everyone and possibly save thousands of lives.

Before he went public with the news, Magic made sure he had plenty of love and support around him, not only from teammates and the rest of the Laker family, but also from his closest former teammates and friends—Kareem, Coop, and Larry Drew. David Stern, the commissioner of the NBA, was called and told about the press conference. He dropped what he was doing in New York and flew to Los Angeles to offer his support to a man he considered to be one of the greatest players and human beings ever to play professional basketball.

When the moment arrived, Magic stood bravely before the cameras and the world. The flashbulbs were exploding in front of him, capturing every emotion on his face as he announced that he had HIV and that he would no longer be playing ball. He did not flinch. He was on a mission. He had a purpose, one that he realized was far more important than any basketball game he had ever played.

He immediately began to help educate Americans, especially young people, by making it clear that having HIV did *not* mean he had developed the AIDS disease. Then he promised to devote himself to the fight against the spread of AIDS and to the search for an eventual cure.

"I'm going to be a spokesman for the HIV virus," he said. "Sometimes you're a little naive . . . and you think something like [acquiring HIV] can never happen to you. It has happened, but I'm going to deal with it. My life will go on," he smiled, "and I'll be a happy man."

The next night, Magic went on the talk show of his good friend, Arsenio Hall. He received a two-minute standing ovation from fans. Magic kept things positive, telling everyone that he wasn't going anywhere, that he was still very much alive and had a lot to live for. He counted his blessings and delivered his message.

Magic's message is one of hope, caution, and love:

1) *Hope* that he can beat the virus and inspire others to beat it as well, to survive until there is a cure.

Still smiling, Earvin "Magic" Johnson appears on national television to educate people about HIV infection and AIDS.

2) *Caution,* especially to young people, about their behavior.

3) *Love* for everyone, and especially for people with AIDS. Love, respect, and support are what people with AIDS need most.

Magic's openness about his condition made an immediate impact. He spoke, and right away people began to listen. Organizations that raise money for AIDS research were overwhelmed with telephone calls from people wanting to know what they could do to help. Thousands of people, all concerned about the spread of AIDS, had themselves tested to make sure that *they* weren't infected and wouldn't give the virus to someone else if they were.

Magic accepted President Bush's offer to be a member of the National Commission on AIDS. From that position, he could not only make a difference in informing young people about AIDS, but he could also be influential in the actions our government takes to combat AIDS.

Through it all, Magic has refused to let anyone feel sorry for him. He hasn't given up on any of his dreams—of raising a family with Cookie, of owning an NBA franchise. Only now he has a new dream: informing people about AIDS in order to help stop its spread.

As cheerful and optimistic as Magic is, people throughout the NBA and the country are deeply concerned, and the outpouring of love has been tremendous. In Phoenix, where the rival Suns play, fans and players signed a huge card saying, "We love you, Magic!" Superstar player Charles Barkley dedicated his entire season to Magic and asked his team, the 76ers, if he could wear Magic's number 32 in his honor. That number, once worn by Hall of Famer

Billy Cunningham, was retired by the 76ers (as Magic's soon will be by the Lakers), but Cunningham said he had no problem with letting Barkley wear it to pay homage to Magic Johnson. Kareem Abdul-Jabbar offered to bring his own number 33 out of retirement and play ball again as a show of support for Magic; Kareem said he would donate his salary to AIDS research.

Even Paul Westhead, the former Laker coach whom Magic didn't want to play for, was in Magic's corner. Coach Westhead (now with the Denver Nuggets) wished Magic good luck and expressed great admiration for his courage.

Outside his family, those most affected by all this have been Magic's teammates. On the flight to Phoenix for their next game, the Lakers boarded the plane. No one sat in Magic's seat. It wasn't something they talked about or decided. It just didn't seem possible that anyone could sit in that seat. That night, before the game, A. C. Green led the fans and players in a prayer for Magic. Some Lakers wept through the national anthem, and none of them could really concentrate on the game. Winning and losing on the hardwood just didn't seem all that important anymore.

Magic may have been on a more important mission than basketball, but he wasn't about to forget his team. The Lakers were still his team, a part of his family, and he wanted to be there for them. He sent a letter to James Worthy to be read at the next game, against the Minnesota Timberwolves, Sunday night at the Forum. The letter was for the Laker fans and players.

Worthy stepped to the public address microphone at center court, his voice full of emotion as he read:

I can't begin to tell you how much strength my family and I are getting from the tremendous support we've received from . . . the fans in Los Angeles, and from so many people everywhere. While I won't be on the court anymore, I want you to know that I'll be here in my usual way: bugging my teammates, coaches, and Jerry West. . . . But I most want to tell you that this is the first day of the rest of our lives. I say this to you fans, because we, the Lakers, need your support more than ever before. I say this to all my teammates because starting now, it's winning time!

The Forum crowd cheered with overwhelming affection after the letter was read, and they kept the support high as the Lakers proved Magic right. It *was* winning time. The Lakers beat the Timberwolves that night, 98–86. Later that week, they went up to Oakland to play the tough Golden State Warriors—and won again.

General Manager Jerry West, himself a Hall of Fame player and one of the greatest guards ever, was asked by reporters about finding a replacement for Magic Johnson. He said,

There's gonna be some kid out there who's gonna be as great as Magic Johnson as a basketball player. No question. There's gonna be some kid out there. He might be ten years old or he might be fifteen years old today. Might not be born. But the problem is, none of them will ever have the charisma he has. This is not only a unique player, but a unique man.

And he'll be able to withstand anything they throw
his way, I promise you.

Sedale Threatt, the new Laker player who was acquired in the off-season to back up Magic Johnson, was now the starting point guard. Asked how he felt about filling Magic's shoes, Threatt said, "No one can fill those shoes." But, inspired by Magic, Threatt has performed brilliantly and is off to the greatest season of his career.

For the Lakers' next home game, against the San Antonio Spurs, Magic Johnson came to the Forum. To wild applause from the crowd, he walked onto the court in his civilian clothes and took a seat on the Laker bench. When the game started, he did everything but play. He coached. He cheered. He gave high fives, he scolded Vlade Divac for dribbling the ball too much. With Magic behind them, the Lakers won nine games in a row, and by the end of 1991 they were still one of the top teams in the NBA. On December 17, Magic joined the Lakers on a road trip to Chicago, where the fans gave him a huge standing ovation—and then Magic cheered the Lakers on to victory against the defending champions.

** ** **

Nobody can really say what the future holds for Earvin "Magic" Johnson. He has promised to be around for a while, to devote himself to his new mission. "I still live," he has said. "I still have fun . . . I'm still me." And perhaps that is his greatest strength. He's a winner—a proven winner—who knows that losing is sometimes part of a much larger victory.

Highlights of Magic's Pro Career
Los Angeles Lakers

- 1979: NBA number-one draft pick, Los Angeles Lakers
- 1980: NBA All-Rookie team selection; Runner-Up Rookie of the Yea
- 1983: Third player in NBA history to record more than 700 points and 700 assists in a single season (Wilt Chamberlain and Oscar Robertson were the other two)
- 1983–1991: First Team All-NBA Guard
- 1984: Most assists in an all-star game (22); NBA Finals single-game assist record (21)
- 1985: NBA Playoffs single-game assist record (record stands at 24)
- 1990: All-Star MVP
- Regular-season MVP: 1986–87, 1988–89, 1989–90
- Western Conference All-Star 11 times
- Most career assists (9,921)
- Played in nine NBA Finals (1980, '82, '83, '84, '85, '87, '88, '89, '91)
- Won five NBA Championships (1980, '82, '85, '87, '88)
- NBA Playoffs MVP three times (1980, '82, '87)
- All-time NBA Playoff assist record (2320)
- *Sport* magazine's NBA Player of the Decade (1980s)

STATS:

Season (year)	Games played in	Field Goal%	Free Throw%	Rebounds (per game)	Assists (per game)	Points (per game)
79–80	77	.530	.810	7.3	7.3	18.0
80–81	37	.532	.760	8.6	8.6	21.6
81–82	78	.537	.760	9.6	9.5	18.6
82–83	79	.548	.800	8.6	10.5	16.8
83–84	67	.565	.810	7.3	13.1	17.6
84–85	77	.561	.843	6.2	12.6	18.3
85–86	72	.526	.871	5.9	12.6	18.8
86–87	80	.522	.848	6.3	12.2	23.9
87–88	72	.492	.853	6.2	11.9	19.6
88–89	77	.509	.910	7.9	12.8	22.5
89–90	79	.480	.890	6.6	11.5	22.3
90–91	79	.477	.906	7.0	12.5	19.4
Totals	874	.521	.848	7.3	11.4	19.7